WCW WCW WCW WCW WCW WCW WCW WCW
CW00687006
SPRING
WCW
STAMPEDE
£4.99
UK only
WCW WCW WCW WCW WCW WCW WC

CONTENTS

WCW ANNUAL 1996

WELCOME

When the publishers of this annual approached me to write it on their behalf, I jumped at the chance. What an opportunity to produce a definitive yearbook about WCW – the finest wrestling organisation in the world.

On the pages following you will find out all of the information about the greatest wrestlers in the sport. You will learn several personal facts about them and their various lifestyles away from wrestling. Best of all, it is packed with new posed shots and unique action photos along with individual biographies.

This book will become a valuable addition to your wrestling library, supplying you with the endless facts and figures that will enable you to truly be considered an expert about WCW.

I hope you enjoy this book as much as I enjoyed writing and photographing it, if you do, you're in for a real treat.

Remember you can keep up with all of the great action from WCW for yourselves on the weekly WCW Worldwide telecasts and by reading WCW Magazine every month.

Enjoy yourselves,
Colin Bowman
Editor,
WCW MAGAZINE

For further information about
WCW MAGAZINE
Send an A4 stamped and self addressed envelope to:
Cell Publishing Ltd
Video House
48 Charlotte St
London W1P 5FN

For further information about
WCW Merchandise
Send a large stamped and self addressed envelope to
PO Box 278
Maidstone
Kent
ME15 6GE

FOR WORLD CHAMPIONSHIP WRESTLING, INC.
President: Dr. Harvey Schiller
Senior Vice President/General Manager: Eric Bischoff
Vice President of Development/Administration: Nick Lambros
Commissioner: Nick Bockwinkel
VP of Production: David Crockett
VP of Sales/Syndication: Rob Garner
VP of International Development/Syndication: Sharon Sidello
Controller: Don Edwards
Director of Marketing Services: Richard Steinberg
Director of PPV/Marketing: Michael Weber
Public Relations Manager: Alan Sharp
Merchandising Co-ordinator: Marco Canales
Editor and Photography: Colin Bowman
Photography: J Stoll TBS
Origination: Newsstand Services
Design: John Derbyshire

Published in Great Britain by World International, an imprint of Egmont Publishing Ltd, Egmont House, PO Box 111, Great Ducie Street, Manchester M60 3BL.

Printed in the United Kingdom.

ISBN 0-7498-2405-0

MACHO
M
MACHO
MAN
RANDY

"Macho Man" SAVAGE

A major force in wrestling for over a decade

One of the most popular and recognisable wrestlers in the world, "Macho Man" Randy Savage followed Hulk Hogan his former friend and foe to WCW after he had failed to find any real competition elsewhere. A major force in wrestling for over a decade, this former two-time World Champion appeared at Starrcade '94 after weeks of teasing whether he would befriend the Hulkster or slap his face. Not only did he extend the hand of friendship to Hogan, but they reformed their successful tag team, "The Monster Maniacs."

Before he became a pro-wrestler, he dreamed of being a major league baseball player. He played in the minor leagues with the Chicago White Sox, the Cincinnati Reds and the St. Louis Cardinals. Since the day he decided to finally hang up his spikes, Savage has found nothing but success in the squared circle.

He wears the wildest outfits and is equally as comfortable wrestling inside the ring or outside of it as an announcer. However, Savage is nothing if not unpredictable and for how long he will content himself without a shot at the World Championship is anyone's guess.

"MACHO MAN" RANDY SAVAGE

Height: 6'1 1/2"
Weight: 245lbs
Birthday: November 15
Hometown: Sarasota, FL
Signature Manoeuvre:
Flying Elbow Drop

Undoubtedly the most exciting new wrestler to appear in WCW for years, this face-painted muscular youngster is already a firm favourite with both children and the young ladies. The electricity that swept through the arena when he first ran down the aisle to be at Hogan's side at Uncensored will long be remembered.

Not a lot is known about him yet, except that he grew up watching the Hulkster and he is undoubtedly his biggest fan and most loyal ally. He is being guided in the ways of Hulkamania by Jimmy Hart and will certainly be a force to be reckoned with for years to come.

RENEGADE

"A force to be reckoned with"

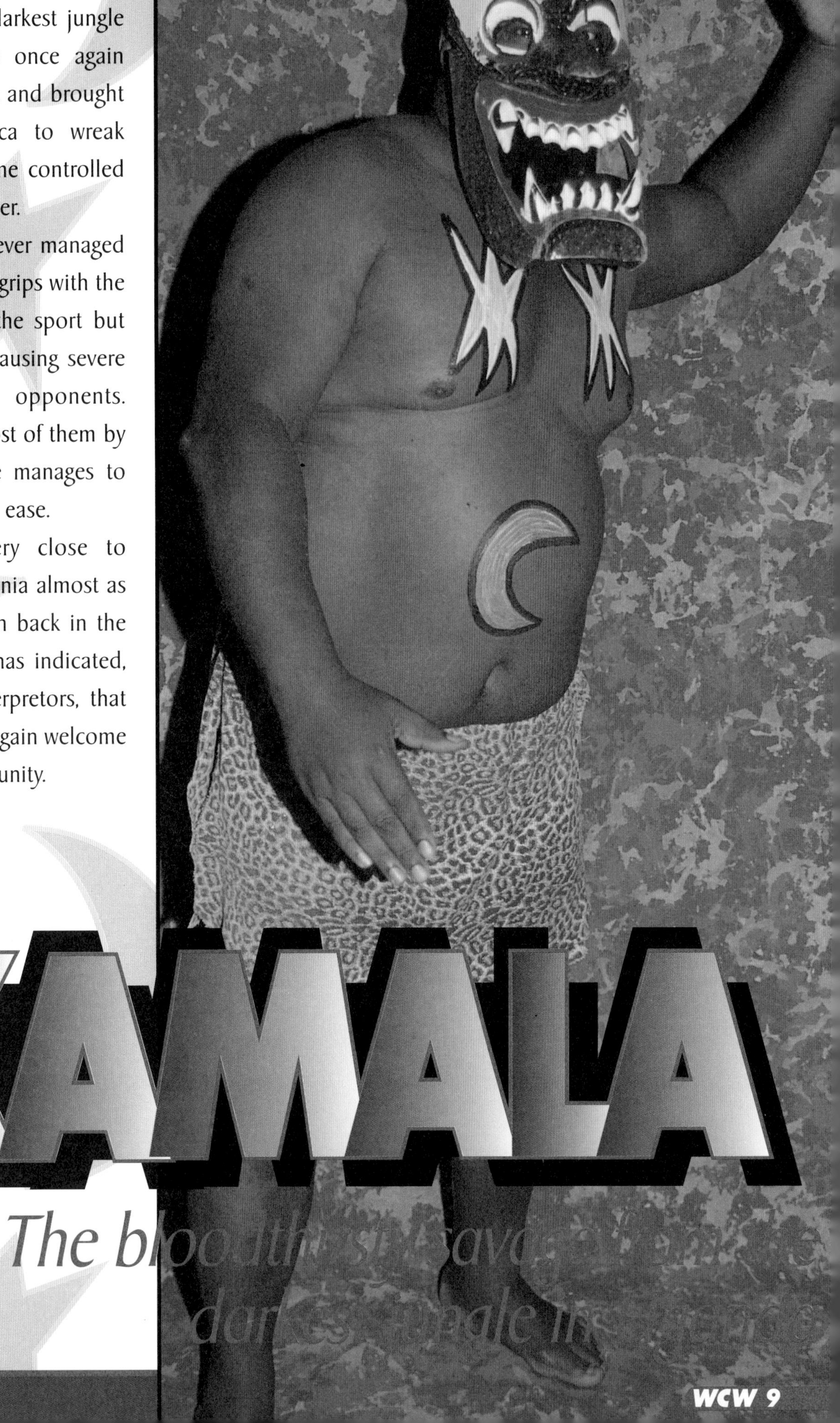

This veteran bloodthirsty savage from the deepest, darkest jungle in Uganda, has once again been sought out and brought back to America to wreak havoc – this time controlled by The Taskmaster.

Kamala has never managed to fully come to grips with the finer points of the sport but he does enjoy causing severe pain to his opponents. Outweighing most of them by over 200lbs, he manages to win with relative ease.

He came very close to ending Hulkamania almost as soon as it began back in the early '80s and has indicated, through his interpretors, that he would once again welcome a similar opportunity.

KAMALA

The b

The NASTY BOYS

Jerry Sags & Brian Knobs

PROFILE

Height: 6'2" & 6'3"
Weight:
310lbs & 320lbs
Birthday:
July 5 & May 6
Hometown:
New York, NY
Signature Manoeuvre:
Elbow Drop & Body Slam
WCW Title Held: World Tag Team Champions (Three times)
9/93, 10/93, 5/95

When Brian Knobs and Jerry Sags roll through a town, children run to the shelter of their parents, fathers grab their guns, and law enforcement officers are put on alert. These are **The Nasty Boys** and their reputation precedes them everywhere they go.

Multi-time holders of the WCW Tag Team Championship title, they love nothing more than a wild brawl inside or outside of the ring. Clad in their wild ring attire, with spiked hair and mouths missing more than a few teeth, they enjoy nothing more than striking fear into beating up and finally humiliating their opponents. Regardless of their wild appearance, no one can doubt the fact that these are talented wrestlers.

Away from the ring they are just as wild and crazy and can often be found indulging in their favourite pastime - the consumption of huge quantities of Big Macs and Whoppers. Their ambition is to "Nasticize" the world and everybody in it.

BOYS
BOYS

Randy 'Pee Wee' Anderson

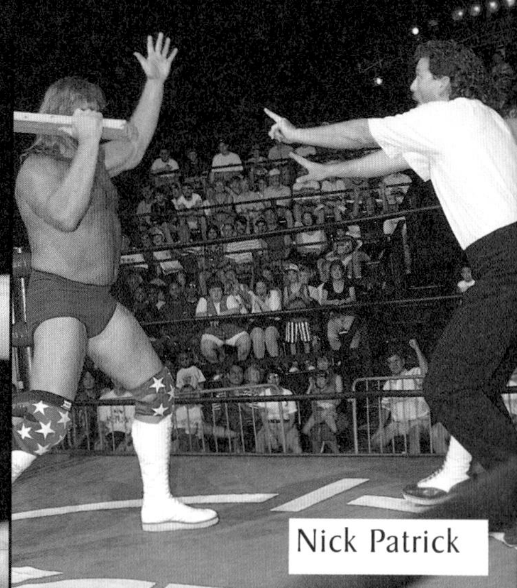

Nick Patrick

Eric Bischoff

Heenan, Schiavone, Bockwinkel

Gene Okerlund

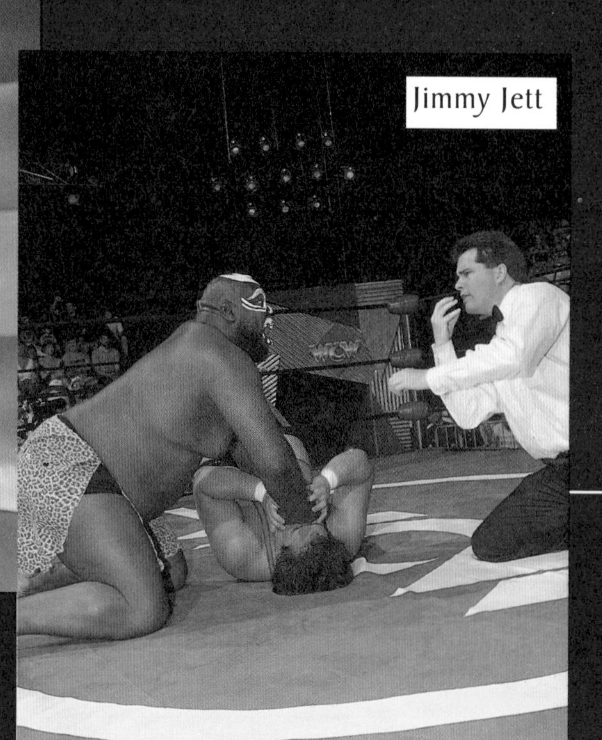

Jimmy Jett

BOBBY "THE BRAIN" HEENAN

Brash and outspoken, Heenan is the sports self proclaimed No.1 broadcast journalist. Unfortunately his reporting is of the standard one would expect to find in the seediest tabloid. Gossip, rumours and innuendoes are the best he can offer. He can be seen and of course heard, on WCW's Saturday Night and Main Event telecasts and every PPV.

MEAN GENE OKERLUND

A true broadcasting legend, Gene combines wit, charisma and an incredible wrestling knowledge. He has been involved with wrestling for over 25 years and has been responsible for breaking several of the sport's biggest stories to the fans.

TONY SCHIAVONE

Tony is sometimes overshadowed by his two more illustrious colleagues, but, more often than not, he will still have his say. The all-round expert on WCW's history, Tony is a mine of obscure and often forgotten information which he uses to make every match he calls just that little bit more special.

ERIC BISCHOFF

The mastermind behind WCW. Eric Bischoff was responsible for Hulk Hogan and "Macho Man" Randy Savage competing in WCW. His visions in both television production and the future of wrestling have led WCW right to the very top. He coined the phrase, "The audience goes where the stars are and the brightest stars are right here in WCW!"

COMMISSIONER NICK BOCKWINKEL

When WCW needed someone who would enforce their rules without fear or favour they enlisted the services of former four times AWA Champion Nick Bockwinkel. During his two years in charge he has proved himself to be an unparalleled mediator, never afraid of making controversial decisions. He has sanctioned both Ric Flair's retirement and return, stripped Vader of the US title and banned Meng from acting as a bodyguard. He has also levied fines totalling hundreds of thousands of dollars against the most persistent offenders. With Nick Bockwinkel at the helm, WCW's fans can rest assured that justice will always be seen to be done.

REFEREES

Randy Pee Wee Anderson
Nick Patrick
Jimmy Jett

The enforcers of law and order in WCW, the referees are the guys the fans love to hate.

Frequently overwhelmed at ringside by the antics of wrestlers, their managers and cohorts, they are sometimes in the wrong place at the wrong time. They are accused of being cheats, blind and lots of things we are unable to print. Despite being protected by the huge fines that are levied if one of them is struck, they are still subject to physical abuse from the wrestlers. Believe them when they say, "The fine is all well and good, but when Vader hits you, the damage is done. He gets a fine he can easily afford, we get a week or more in hospital."

Life definitely doesn't seem fair when you're a referee!

REFEREES & COMMENTATORS

ATTENTION! EYES FRONT! No talking in the ranks, you undisciplined civilians!

The pride of the United States Marine Corps has entered WCW with an attitude resembling a pack of hungry dogs. His mission – to kick butt and then go back and do it again. A multiple holder of the Armed Forces wrestling championship, "Pitbull" enjoys subjecting all of his opponents to his boot-camp assault. He has an incredible array of manoeuvre at his disposal, including his dreaded "Code Red" the most feared submission hold in WCW.

Sgt. Craig PITTMAN

The Martial Arts Master...

MENG

When Commissioner Bockwinkel banned Meng from his bodyguard duties, he couldn't have guessed what an incredible force of nature he was unleashing on WCW's unsuspecting wrestlers.

A master of every martial art and with a inner knowledge of the mysteries of the Orient, Meng has been most formidable.

Guided by his close friend and manager, Colonel Robert Parker, Meng's brutal style has resulted in several young wrestlers being carried out of the ring on a stretcher. He now holds the psychological advantage over his opponents and is looking forward to challenging for EVERY title available in WCW.

PROFILE

STING™

Height: 6'3"
Weight: 252lbs
Birthday: March 20
Hometown: Venice Beach, CA
Signature Manoeuvre: Scorpion Deathlock
WCW Title Held: World Heavyweight Champion: (3 times) 7/90, 2/92, 3/93
World TV Champion: 3/89
US Heavyweight Champion: 8/91, 6/95
European Cup Winner: 3/94

Combine charismatic charm, flamboyant costumes and face paint along with incredible athletic ability and you have WCW's most popular wrestler - Sting. This Californian native has won countless WCW titles, including three reigns as World Heavyweight Champion. He also won the inaugural European Cup in 1994 and is now undoubtedly in the prime of his career.

It was all so different when he was younger. Painfully shy, he was encouraged to participate in sports. As his confidence grew, he pushed himself to the limit, often taking many risks at the expense of his body...the same kind of determination that has brought him so much success in his career.

Outside of the ring, Sting's heart is as big as his biceps. He is actively involved with many charities including the Starlight Foundation. In the words of the Stinger, "The feeling is overwhelming when you see a look of joy come over a child's face."

When Sting is not wrestling or brightening some child's day, he spends his time weight training, body surfing, water skiing or riding on his Harley Davidson.

STING™

WCW's most popular wrestler

PROFILE

Height: 6'
Weight: 222lbs
Birthday: May 22
Hometown: California
Signature Manoeuvre:
Flying Headscissors
WCW Titles Held:
World Tag Team Champion 3/93
Light Heavyweight Champion (twice)
10/91, 2/92
US Tag Team Champion 2/90

The premier aerialist in the sport, Brian continues to astound opponents and fans alike with his ever developing arsenal of high risk and higher flying manoeuvres. This heartthrob has dominated the world's lightweight division ever since he gave up his American Football career with the Cincinnati Bengals. He has also proved he can hold his own against his larger and heavier peers.

Still young and ambitious, Brian is still seeking to add to his already impressive honour roll.

Flyin' Brian PILLMAN

STUNNING Steve Austin

"Tipped to be the biggest star"

Arrogant, cocky, flashy and loud. These are just four of the adjectives that can be used to describe Austin. He is also very talented. It is very rare that a wrestler comes along who possesses the talents to be as equally successful in singles and tag team action. But Steve is no ordinary wrestler. Since he won his first title in WCW a mere fortnight after he arrived, Austin has won every belt except for the World Championship. He is confident that if he is ever given a shot that belt will also be his.

Widely tipped to be the biggest star in the next millennium, Stunning Steve knows he has time on his side and right now he is patiently contemplating his next move towards the top.

PROFILE

Height: 6'2"
Weight: 252lbs
Birthday: December 18
Hometown: Hollywood, CA
Signature Manoeuvre:
Stun-Gun
WCW Titles Held:
World Tag Team Champion
3/93
World TV Champion (twice)
6/91, 5/92
US Champion (twice)
12/93, 9/94

DAS WUNDERKIND ALEX WRIGHT

Germany's youngest ever pro-wrestle

PROFILE

DAS WUNDERKIND
ALEX WRIGHT
Height: 6' 4"
Weight: 216lbs
Birthday: May 17
Hometown: Nuremburg, Germany
Signature Manoeuvre: Reverse Cross-Body

He is known as "Das Wunderkind" because of his tough and eager personality. Alex was discovered by WCW officials in March 1994 while they were on a tour of Germany. They were so impressed by his exceptional wrestling skills and the fact that he was so young and eager to learn.

Alex is a second generation wrestler, the son of famous English wrestler Steve Wright, who emigrated to Germany two decades ago. Alex followed his father into a mat career starting with a very successful amateur career. He became Germany's youngest ever pro-wrestler and the rest, as they say, is history.

Alex has designs on becoming one of the youngest WCW Champions in history but realizes he has much to learn as he works his way up the rankings. Patience is one of his virtues and he knows his time will come if he stays focused on the task ahead.

Bellowing his battle cry of "Hooooo!," armed with a trusty two-by-four and carrying the American flag, Duggan won't win any awards for scientific grappling. From the opening bell, this barrel chested brawler pulverises his opponents with an uncomplicated range of power moves. He is fiercely defensive of America and her allies, taking personally any insult against them. It is this patriotic streak that has involved him in many memorable feuds where his never-say-die attitude has carried him to victory.

A New York state amateur wrestling champion and a successful collegiate football player, Duggan took his skills to the NFL where he played for the Atlanta Falcons. He then adapted his gridiron prowess for use in the squared circle and he has enjoyed a solid transition to a mat career. His biggest moment came when he won the US Championship in 1994, but unfortunately lost it to Vader.

With a lifestyle as straight forward as his wrestling, Hacksaw has never forgotten his humble roots or the importance of his fans. It is that attitude which has made him one of the most beloved wrestlers in the world today. He is considered by everyone to be the "People's Champion."

HACKSAW Jim Duggan

The People's Champion

Likes & Dislikes of WCW WRESTLERS

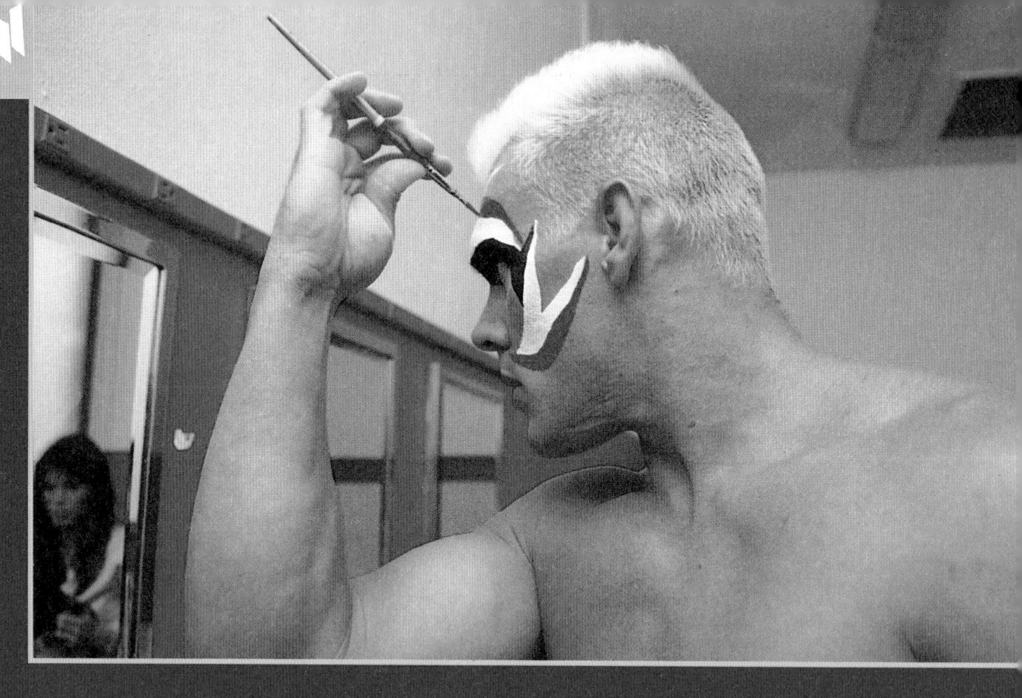

We asked our top WCW Wrestlers some general questions about their likes and dislikes of various things:-

Favourite Wrestler

Least Favourite Wrestler

Favourite food

Car in garage

Favourite film

Favourite actor/actress

Favourite hobby

Birthsign

Major dislike

Favourite Country visite

Favourite Band

We received some amazing answers. See for yourself

STUNNING STEVE AUSTIN
Dory Funk Jr.
Flyin' Brian
Cajun
Jeep
Cool Hand Luke
Bela Lugosi
Hunting
Sagittarius
9 to 5'ers (Losers)
None
Alice in Chains

RENEGADE
Hulk Hogan
Ric Flair
Any food
Viper
Mr. Nanny
Hulk Hogan
Weightlifting
Libra
Lying
Japan
Metallica

LORD STEVEN REGAL
Earl Robert
Any American
Roast Beef & Yorkshire Pudding
Aston Martin DB6
Henry V
Terry Thomas
Fine arts, Herpetology
Taurus
Americans
South Africa
Royal Philharmonic Orchestra

TASKMASTER
Myself
Myself
Spinach
Harley
Beyond the Valley of the Dolls
Steve Reeves
Taxidermist
Scorpio
The English
Nova Scotia
Glen Miller

STING
"Macho Man" Randy Savage
Big Bubba Rogers
Mexican
Dodge Viper
Action Movies
Nicholas Cage
Pisces
Humidity
England
Rock 'n Roll

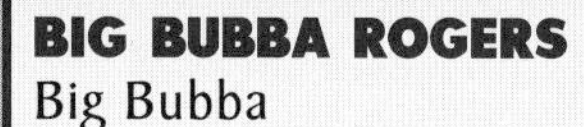

BIG BUBBA ROGERS
Big Bubba
Sting
Grilled Chicken
Truck
Texas Chainsaw Massacre
Sandra Bullock
Beating up other wrestlers
Taurus
People who think they're better than other people
Australia
Guns & Roses

SGT. CRAIG PITTMAN
Myself
Hulk Hogan
Steak
Land Cruiser
Few Good Men
Jack Nicholson
Flying
Libra
Undisciplined Civilians
Sweden
Bach

DDP
Myself
Dave Sullivan
Don Pirignon & Chato Briants
Lamberjeanie
Pulp Fiction
Kim Basinger
Spending Money
Aries
Peasants who ask me for money
Sweden
Aerosmith

FLYIN' BRIAN
Buddy Rogers
Ric Flair
Sushi
Accura
Reservoir Dogs
Al Pacino
Coin collecting
Gemini
Traffic
Germany
Candlebox

MARCUS BAGWELL
Sting
Vader
Steak
Mercedes
48 Hours
Tom Cruise
Snow skiing
Capricorn
Bad Movies
England
Live

ARN ANDERSON
Me
Hulk Hogan
Broiled Seafood
Mercedes
One Flew Over the Cuckoo's Nest
Jack Nicholson
Working Out
Virgo
Fat Women
Switzerland
Led Zeppelin

HACKSAW JIM DUGGAN
Hulkster
Vader
Hot Dog
Pick-up truck
True Lies
John Wayne
Handgun shooting
Capricorn
Rude People
England
Clint Black

VADER
Arn Anderson
Hulk Hogan
Double Cheese Whopper
Rolls Royce
Fist of the North Star
Schwarzenegger
Four Wheel Driving
Taurus
Hulk Hogan
Georgia
Led Zeppelin

JERRY SAGS
Brian Knobs
Mad Dog Vachon
Philly Cheesesteaks
'54 Chevy
Animal House
Dennis Hopper
Boating
Cancer
People that aren't Nasty
Germany
Rolling Stones

DAVE SULLIVAN
Hulkster
Ric Flair
Strawberry Pie
Plymouth
King Lion
Forrest Gump
Taking my Prayers, Saying my Vitamins and Working out
Do I have one?
People that aren't nice
Europe
Brooks Garth

HARLEM HEAT
Booker T & Stevie Ray
Everybody who ain't with us
Neckbone
Corvette Z28
Terminator 1 & 2
Sidney Poitier
Beating people up
Leo Pisces
Media
Virgin Islands
Public Enemy

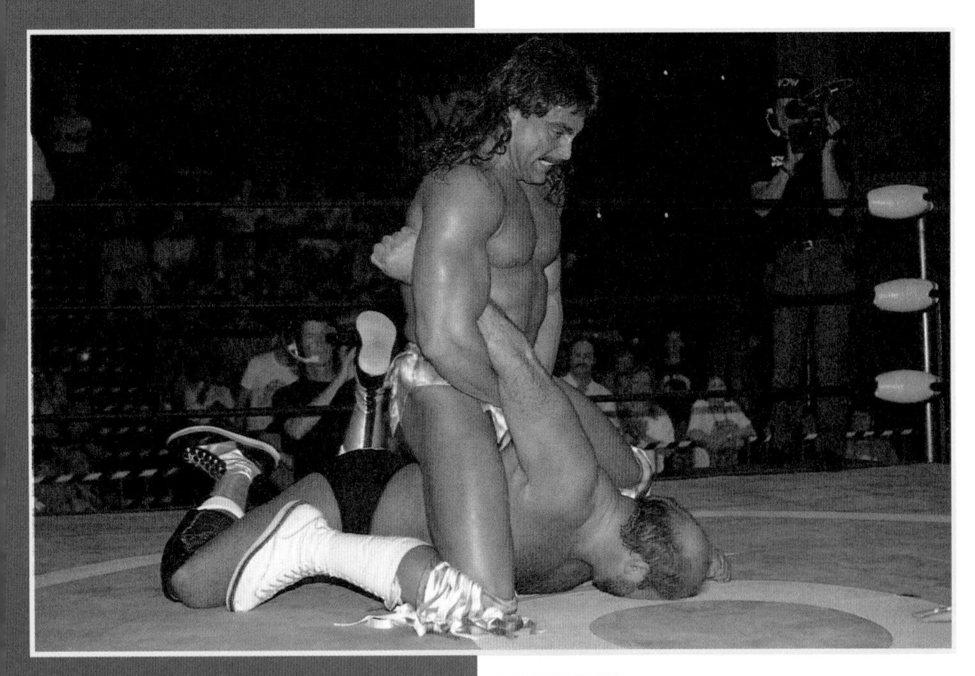

The most outrageous wrestler in WCW history is, without a doubt, Johnny B. Badd. Behind that devastating "Tutti Frutti" left hook is a former US Boxing Team member and a five-time state boxing champion. There is no question that this 6-foot, 235-pound, Little Richard look-alike is one of the hottest wrestlers in the world today.

Johnny is spreading his campaign of "Stay clean, you know what I mean" across the country. He talks to children and expresses the importance of finishing school and staying away from drugs. In the words of the Badd-man, "Don't be a fool, stay in school. If you're not on the honour roll, you're not going to be on the payroll." In addition, Johnny visits children's hospitals in an effort to bring hope and courage to them and to let them know he cares.

Whenever his schedule permits, the former WCW Television Champion enjoys aerobics, weight lifting, signing autographs and meeting people. His own personal mantra is, "Keep your body and mind clean and always strive to be the best that you can be!"

Johnny B. BADD

Stay clean, You know what I mean

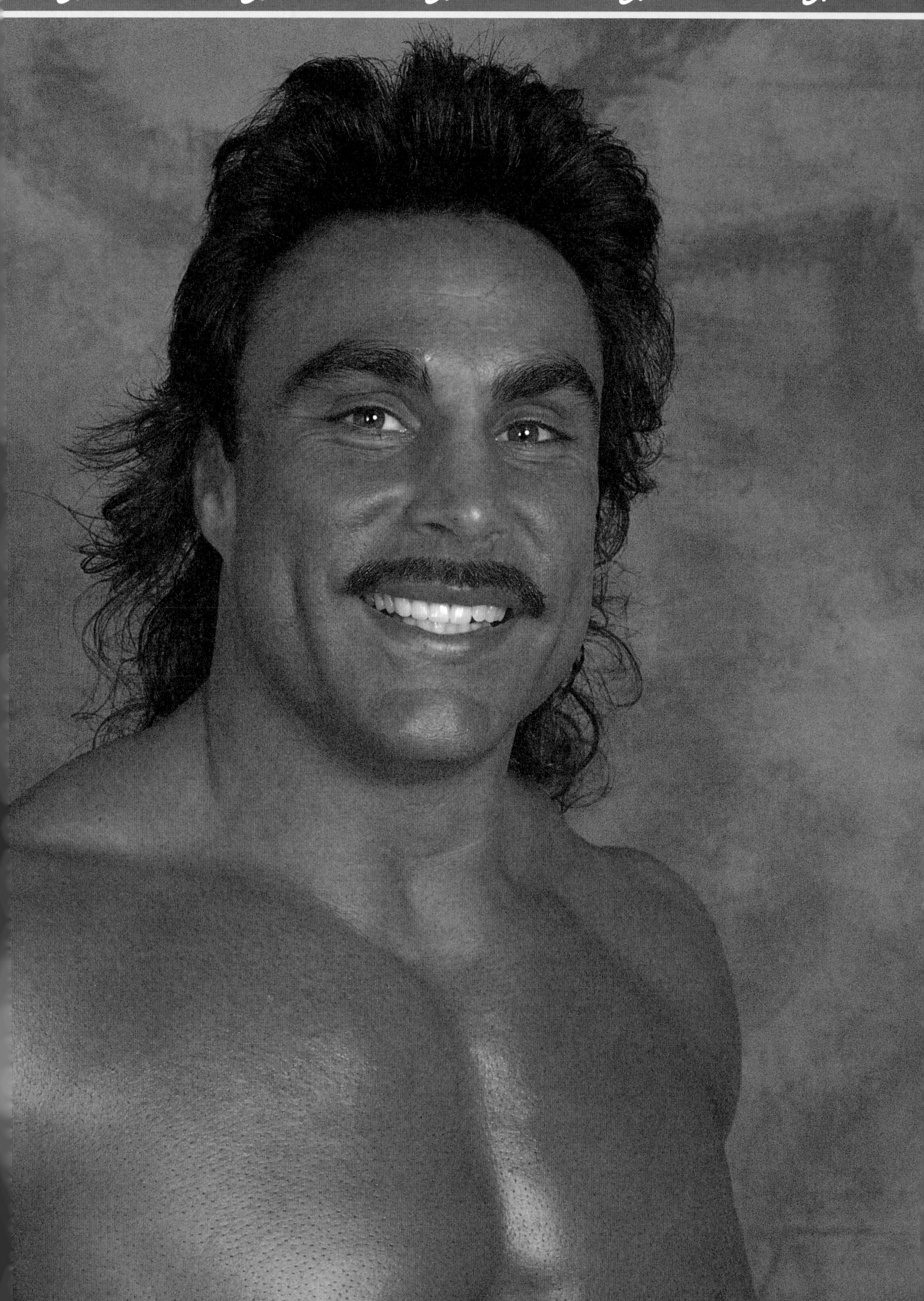

Blue BLOODS

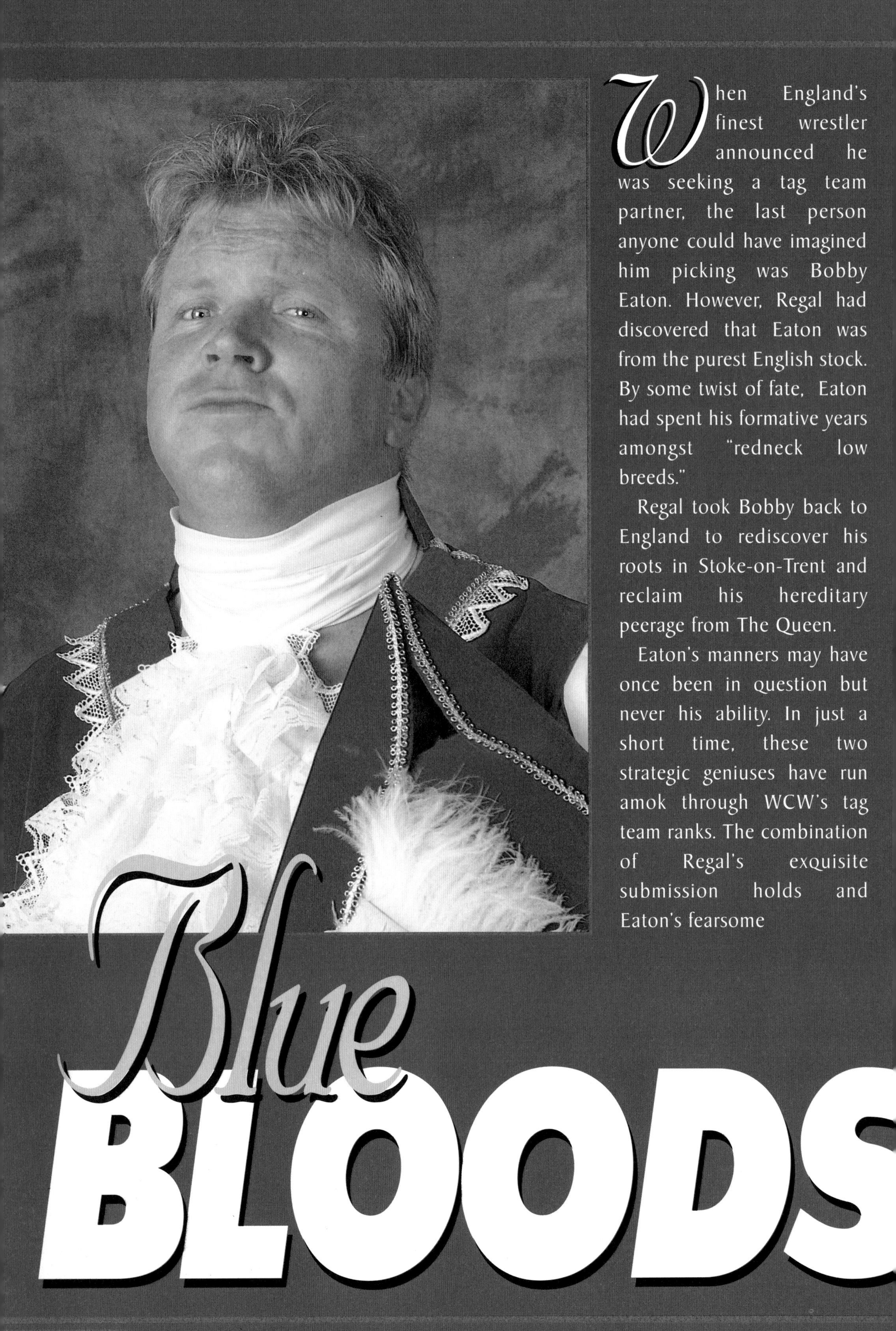

When England's finest wrestler announced he was seeking a tag team partner, the last person anyone could have imagined him picking was Bobby Eaton. However, Regal had discovered that Eaton was from the purest English stock. By some twist of fate, Eaton had spent his formative years amongst "redneck low breeds."

Regal took Bobby back to England to rediscover his roots in Stoke-on-Trent and reclaim his hereditary peerage from The Queen.

Eaton's manners may have once been in question but never his ability. In just a short time, these two strategic geniuses have run amok through WCW's tag team ranks. The combination of Regal's exquisite submission holds and Eaton's fearsome

'Tower of London' legdrop have the sports top pundits convinced that the World Tag Team Championship is not very far from this duo's grasp.

As for the Earl's new found status outside the ring...he's taken to it like the proverbial duck to water and is now quite possibly even more arrogant and anti-American than his pompous partner.

Lord Regal & Earl Robert

On June 4, 1994, World Championship Wrestling and Hulk Hogan surprised the planet with a gift to fans all over the world - the Hulkster's return to the ring! This move represented the greatest acquisition in wrestling history and was the crowning jewel in the incredible array of talent competing in WCW.

His comeback was firmly etched in the wrestling annals on July 17, when the Hulkster won the world's oldest and most prestigious title by conquering his long-time nemesis, Ric Flair, to become the WCW World Heavyweight Champion.

The Real American Hero

WCW™ HULK

To simply say that Hulk Hogan is the most famous wrestler in the world would be an understatement. No other wrestler has impacted pop culture like Hogan. With his signature bandanna, fiery eyes, blond moustache and rippling biceps tearing through his yellow t-shirt, the Hulkster is a charismatic, larger-than-life persona who has become a genuine American icon.

At 6'7", 275-pounds, Hogan has always done things in a big way. "Hulkamania" was already running wild," when he claimed his first World Championship in 1984. Following that he ignited the spark that propelled wrestling into a worldwide phenomenon throughout the 80's and 90's. During this period he appeared on the cover of "Sports Illustrated" magazine, garnered four more world titles and competed in jam-packed arenas and stadia all over the planet. In one of his most memorable bouts, Hogan body-slammed his way to victory against the 7'4",

HOGAN™

WCW™
HOGAN

HULKSTER™

500 pound Andre the Giant before a capacity crowd in the Pontiac Silverdome. This event surpassed all previous indoor attendance records including those set by the Pope and The Rolling Stones, when over 93,000 people witnessed the spectacle.

There is more to Hogan than just being a wrestler. He has starred in many films including *"Suburban Commando," "Mr. Nanny"* and *"Rocky III"* and recently had the lead role in the successful syndicated television series *"Thunder in Paradise."* He has even released his first music album this year - *"American*

Made," which has enjoyed huge success in the USA and Europe.

Hulk is a "real American hero," adored by millions of fans, especially children. This adoration is mutual as Hulk, despite his busy schedule, always finds time to visit ailing children all over the world. He is an active participant in the Make-A-Wish Foundation of which he is the number one requested celebrity. He is also involved with the Pediatric AIDS Center, Special Olympics and Starlight Foundation.

It is in the ring, however, where Hulk has his greatest following. His battles in 1995 against Vader, Butcher, Avalanche and Ric Flair have enhanced his status as a legend. As long as his little "Hulkamaniacs" continue to say their prayers, take their vitamins and train hard, Hulk will continue to battle for truth, justice and the American way.

This legendary, brutal, but scientific wrestler just seems to be like a good wine, getting better with age. His reflexes may have slowed down, but his brain and body are still as sharp as ever.

Once again he is focussing on singles competition and has his old foe, Hulk Hogan, squarely in his sights. In the early '80s their feud tore up the whole of the United States as they faced off in front of some of the largest ever crowds to watch professional wrestling. Armed with the deadliest piledriver in sport, who would wish to give odds against him garnering even more titles before he is ready to call it a day?

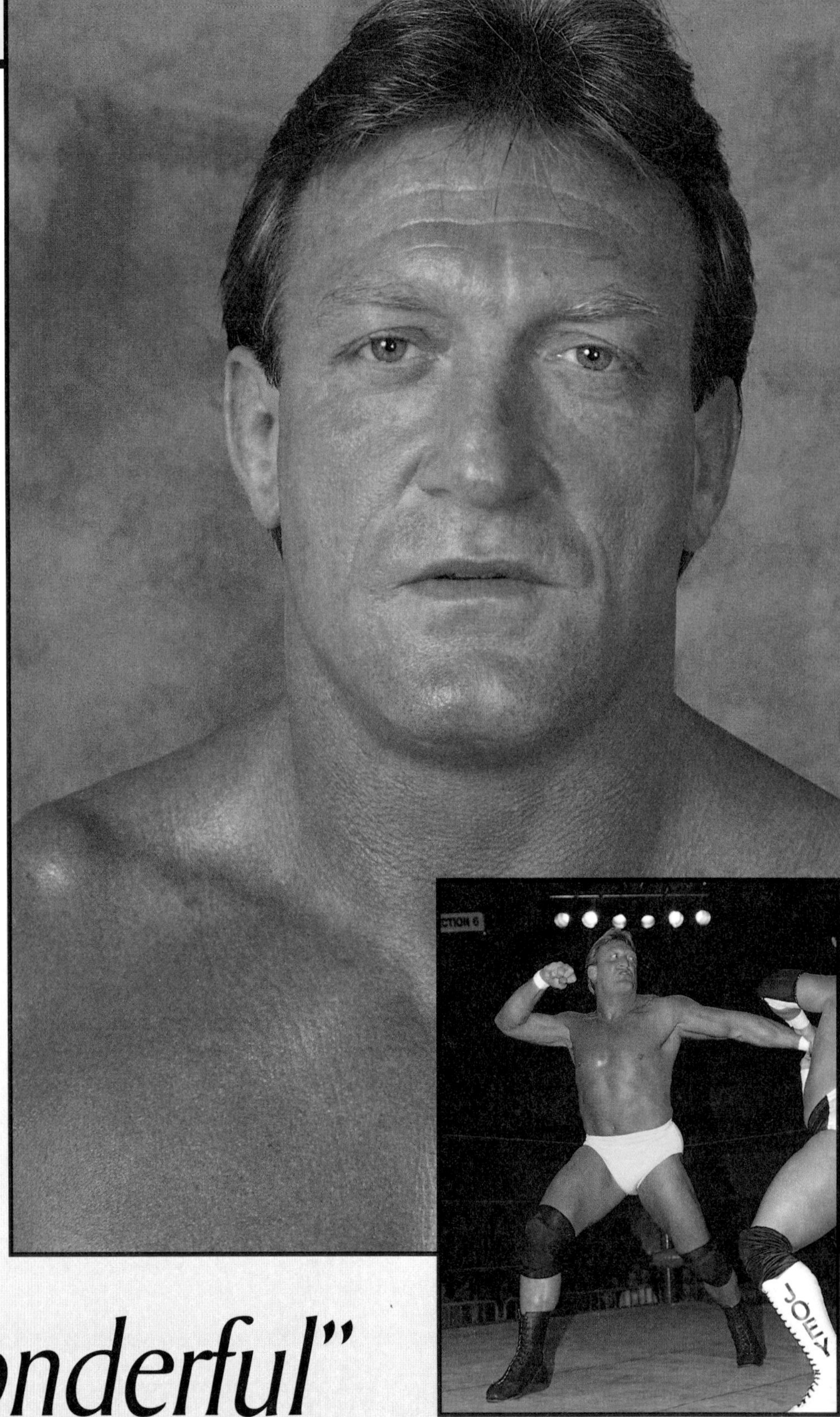

"Mr Wonderful" PAUL ORNDORFF

......."getting better with age"

You won't find two more ornery critters than Bunkhouse Buck and Dirty Dick Slater. Colonel Parker's mercenaries enter the ring with just one thing in mind...the destruction of their opponents in the shortest possible time. They often go straight at it, pummelling opponents with lefts and rights, kicking and gouging. The agony doesn't end at the final bell as hapless wrestlers are bound and hog-tied and subjected to even more punishment. Matches involving this pair, should carry a warning that states – "Any similarity to wrestling is purely coincidental!"

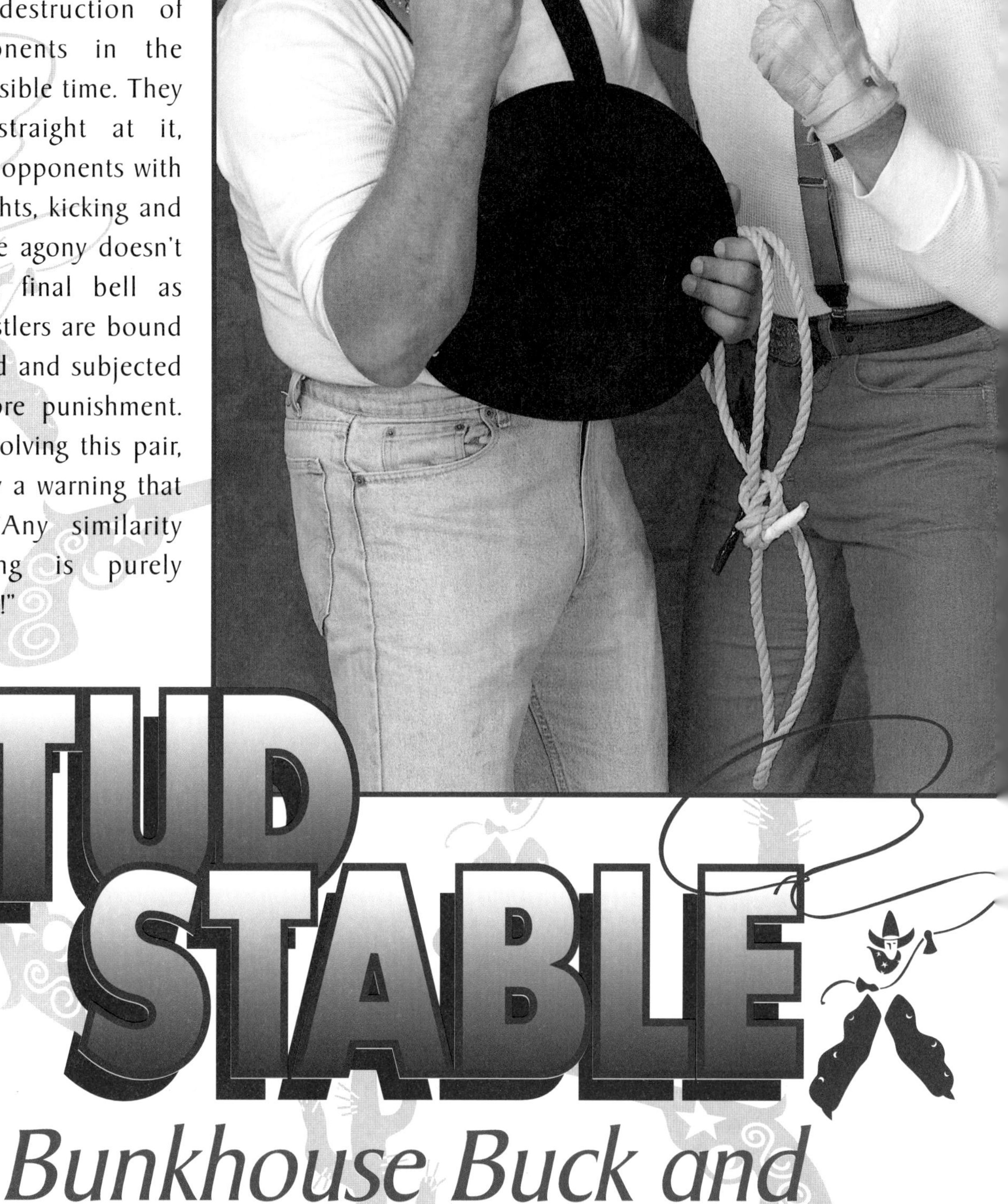

STUD STABLE

Bunkhouse Buck and Dirty Dick Slater

Behind The SCENES

When you switch on your TV to watch WCW Worldwide or to view a video from the latest shows, do you ever wonder why it looks so great?

Well, this is our tribute to all the highly skilled and unsung technical staff who work tirelessly behind the scenes to make sure WCW remains the number one wrestling organisation in the world.

It takes over 200 technicians, engineers, equipment operators, audio and video directors, cameramen, grips, secretaries and assistants to put on each of these events. For a major event like Starrcade or Halloween Havoc, these specialists arrive in town 36 hours before the big show. Under the watchful eye of David Crockett, WCW's Vice President of Production, the lighting rigs and thousands of lights and strobes are set up along with the ring and the arena seating. The complex pyrotechnics are tested and armed and endless miles of camera and lighting cables are laid. The transmission dishes are then aligned to the satellites so that the broadcast can be seen all over America.

There are of course back-ups for every piece of equipment. Just imagine how intolerable it would be if anything went wrong with a live telecast and millions of watching viewers were deprived of one second of pleasure. Craig Leathers, the director is ultimately in charge of how the final product appears on your

screen. Sitting in the control truck surrounded by banks of monitors it is his job to make sure that the cameramen, keep up with all of the action. In a sport that is as unpredictable as wrestling, he feels those WCW technicians are the best in the world and when he gets a moment to view the final footage he is very proud of their efforts...even if at times he may feel like pulling his hair out when things don't always go to plan.

However glamorous being involved behind the scenes of WCW may seem, there are huge sacrifices to be made. For example at Starrcade '94 in Nashville, the crew rolled into town on Christmas Eve and had to spend the Christmas holiday separated from their families and friends setting up the arena and unloading the eight large articulated lorries that carry the kit. This story is repeated several times throughout the year, just so that WCW fans around the whole world can enjoy the best family entertainment anywhere.

So, next time you are enjoying the antics of Hulk Hogan, Sting, Randy Savage and all the others stars in WCW, spare a thought for those unsung heroes who make it all possible.

Like his violent natural disaster namesake, Avalanche crashed his way into the ranks of WCW with 505 pounds of crushing force. His attack on Hulk Hogan made an immediate impact on the competitive landscape in WCW. Possessing immense size and unbelievable speed, this former tag team champion and undefeated Sumo competitor (24-0) has shown he cannot be taken lightly, quite literally. His past misdemeanours include breaking Hulk Hogan's ribs and he has also left a large path strewn with broken bodies in his wake.

Avalanche has a tremendous amateur background. He was a five time Canadian National Champion and in 1983 he won the Junior World Wrestling Championship, the first ever world wrestling title held by a Canadian.

With strong ties to Kevin Sullivan and Big Bubba, Avalanche will do anything in his power to sweep aside the opposition and become WCW's greatest force of nature. He dares anyone to stand in the ring after he has issued the Avalanche Warning..

AVALANCHE

WCW's Greatest Force of Nature

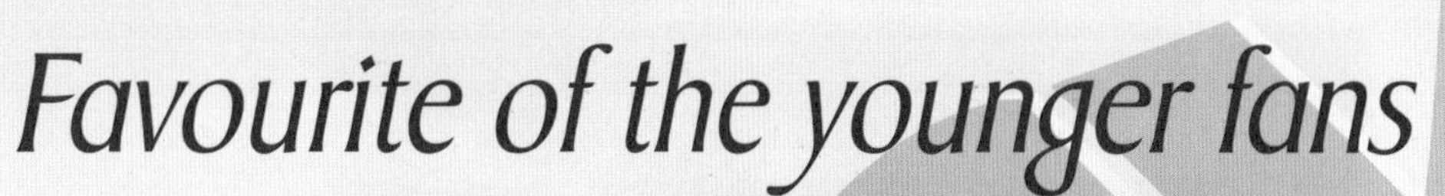

Favourite of the younger fans

DAVE SULLIVAN

There has never been a kinder, gentler and nicer wrestler than Dave Sullivan – but then again there haven't been any as naive.

He spells his name Evad and he is always getting things mixed up, much to the chagrin of his fellow wrestlers.

Brave as a lion, he never backs down from any challenge, even facing up to his psychopathic brother in a series of hard fought matches earlier this year.

Dave, is accompanied to the ring by his rabbit Ralph. He is a firm favourite with the younger fans in WCW who can identify with many of lifes confusions which he continually faces.

Diamond Dallas PAGE

The man who has it all!

The richest, most handsome, best dressed, most talented wrestling superstar and announcer of all time. No, we didn't say that, we just gave you an insight into DDP's own view of himself.

Rarely seen without a huge cigar, accompanied by the beautiful – if not terribly naive – Diamond Doll and his bodyguard Max Muscle, DDP enjoys nothing more than spending his time shopping, gambling and sneering at the peasants who ask him for money.

Although he is a talented wrestler, there always appears to be too many distractions and playthings surrounding him that keep him from any major success in the squared circle.

As he says, "I have it all, money and looks, why should I work hard for a gold belt when I can just go out and buy a hundred?" This is not an attitude that has earned him any respect from other wrestlers or the fans, although they do cast a jealous eye toward the Diamond Doll.

Stars & Stripes are undoubtedly the most exciting young tag team in the world today. Marcus Bagwell is a former all-county and all-state football and baseball player from Marietta, GA. This former "rookie of the year," wrestled throughout his high school career while dreaming breaking into the professional ranks. For a long time Marcus gained as much publicity for his good looks and muscular physique as his wrestling ability. Now he is proving that he is no pushover and is getting to live out his dream in the squared circle.

His partner, The Patriot, honed his not inconsiderable skills wrestling in Japan. Clad in red, white and blue from head to foot - including his symbolic mask - he is well on his way to becoming America's newest wrestling superhero.

Ideally suited, these former WCW Tag Team Champions share many common bonds. They train long and hard at the gym to maintain their incredible physiques. Their clean living and respectable lifestyles have made them the perfect role models for the youth of today.

Marcus Bagwell & The Patriot

PROFILE

VADER

Height: 6'5"
Weight: 450lbs
Birthday: May 14
Hometown: Rocky Mountains, CO
Signature Manoeuvre: Vadersault
WCW Titles Held: World Heavyweight Champion: (3 times) 7/92, 12/92, 3/93
US Champion 12/94

Despite his outward appearance, Vader is an incredible athlete with extensive football experience including a four-year stint in the NFL with the LA Rams. His conditioning has made him the most agile super heavyweight ever to compete in the sport. He is legendary for his dreaded top rope Vadersault, an amazing manoeuvre when executed by wrestlers half his size.

He is the only wrestler in history to have held 11 world titles spanning three continents, including three stints as WCW World Heavyweight Champion. Add to these a WCW US Championship and you can see why Vader was installed for most of 1995 as the No.1 contender to the World title.

With a reputation for being merciless and a trail of broken bodies left in his wake, it is no surprise to learn that his favourite saying is, "The name of the game is PAIN and nobody plays as well as VADER!" No WCW Champion can ever feel safe while this behemoth is on the loose and looking to add to his tally of titles.

The name of the game is PAIN and nobody plays as well as

VADER

At 6'6" and 330-pounds, Big Bubba Rogers has been known to throw his weight around. Formerly known as the "man who stood for law and order," he has turned his back on the values he once protected. Big Bubba now stands for the only right way - his way!

Sporting braces, suit and fedora hat, his slick looks are more akin to a fast-talking (albeit a very large) country lawyer. His ring strategy is rarely concerned with technical or scientific manoeuvres. He prefers to rely on simplistic, straight forward brute force. His aggressive methods often just pummel his opponents into submission...his preferred method of finishing a match.

As a former bodyguard, prison guard and Guardian Angel, Bubba draws upon a wide range of experience when exacting punishment. He has also become a constant nemesis of Commissioner Nick Bockwinkel and Sting. Bubba has declared, "I have gone back to my roots and it won't be long before I'll be sporting the championship gold!"

BIG BUBBA ROGERS

"the man who stood for law & order"

PROFILE

Height: 6'
Weight: 249lbs
Birthday: September 20
Hometown: Minneapolis, MN
Signature Manoeuvre:
Spine Buster
WCW Titles Held:
World Tag Team Champion-(five times) 9/78, 4/88, 9/91, 1/92, 8/93
World TV Champion-(four times)
1/86, 1/90, 1/91, 1/95

THE ENFORCER

Arn Anderson

Arn. Even his name is a snarl. This unsurpassed wrestling master, whose style can vary from street tough brawling to scientific, is one of the most respected grapplers in the sport today. Arn combines a genius for ring strategy with devastating finishing holds, such as his Spine Buster and DDT, to tear through the competition.

Arn grew up as part of a famous wrestling family and so inevitably he was drawn into the sport. He is the consummate tag team wrestler having won the World Tag Team Championship on five occasions. That should not detract from his ability in singles competition as he has also won the World Television title on a record-breaking four occasions.

Arn is frequently found at the side of his close friend and fellow founder of The Four Horsemen, Ric Flair, often sacrificing personal success to see that his cohort remains at the top of the sport.

The nickname, "Enforcer," has been well earned. Not too many wrestlers queue up to face Arn and when they do they often regret it. He frequently advises, "Know your strengths and never let an opponent know your weaknesses!"

PROFILE

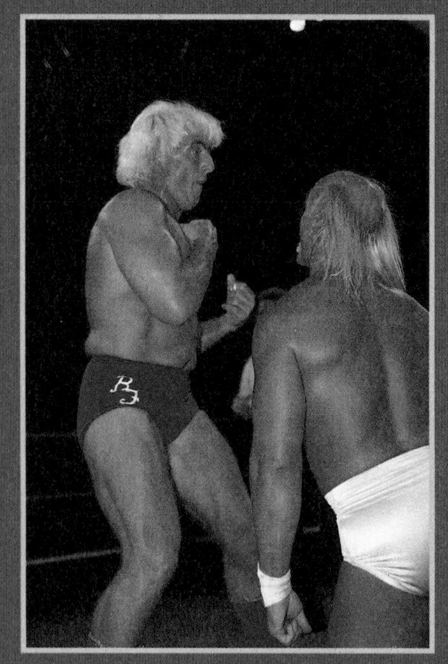

Rf

Height: 6'1"
Weight: 240lbs
Birthday: February 25
Hometown: Charlotte, NC
Signature Manoeuvre:
Figure Four Leglock
WCW Titles Held:
World Heavyweight
Champion (11 times)
9/81, 11/83, 3/84, 5/84,
8/86, 11/87, 5/89, 1/91,
5/91, 7/93, 12/93
World Tag Team
Champion: (3 times)
2/77, 11/77, 9/79
US Heavyweight
Champion: (5 times)
10/77, 8/78, 5/79,
4/80, 11/80

When he lost the now infamous cage retirement match at Halloween Havoc 1994 to Hulk Hogan, the world assumed it had seen the last of Ric Flair. Given the huge ego and vanity that is an indelible part of Flair's make up, it came as no surprise when he began to harangue Hulk Hogan and Randy Savage until their pleas for his reinstatement were finally rubber stamped by Commissioner Nick Bockwinkel.

Since his return the former 11-time World Heavyweight Champion has shown he hasn't lost a step. "The dirtiest player in the game," still is. The seven month lay-off did nothing to dull his skills. Instead he has returned with the old fires burning deep within as he searches for both his 12th title and the way to bring about the end of Hulkamania.

Flair may be classed as a veteran, but to write him off would be premature. Remember he has avenged every previous title defeat and now once again he has Hulk Hogan in his sights.

"Nature Boy" RIC

FLAIR

Suave, Sophisticated and MEAN !

PROFILE

BUTCHER
Height: 6' 3"
Weight: 255lbs
Birthday: April 21
Hometown: San Francisco, CA
Signature Manoeuvre: Sleeperhold

A man who now stands alone. He butchered his longtime friendship with Hulk Hogan and then fell out with his fellow partners in terror, The Three Faces of Fear.

Butcher hasn't been the same since that fateful parasailing accident in 1990. He is in great physical shape, but his psyche undoubtedly suffered. This makes him all the more dangerous and he is trusted by no one.

He recently said, "If I'm alone, then so be it. I'm tough and can look after myself. Woe betide any wrestlers who have crossed me in the past or who get in my face in the future!"

BUTCHER

.....Trusted by no one

TASKMASTER

PROFILE

TASKMASTER
Height: 5'9"
Weight: 247lbs
Birthday: October 26
Hometown: Daytona Beach, FL
Signature Manoeuvre:
Double Stomp
WCW Titles Held: World Tag Team Champion 5/94
US Tag Team Champion 12/88

This psychotic maniac from "The Gates of Hate" has been terrorising his opponents for well over a decade. He shows no mercy from the moment he steps inside the ring and has even been known to use hammers, spikes and scissors in his pursuit of victory.

A twisted genius, with the highest IQ in wrestling, he has throughout the years set up several cults, convincing other weaker minded wrestlers to carry out his biddings. At this time he has unveiled some strange mystical markings on his forehead and his latest followers are Avalanche and Kamala.

No one has ever been able to fathom out the way his mind works, it's obvious that titles don't interest him, so what does? Money? Power? Or perhaps...your MINDS!

WCW
WORLD

HARLEM HEAT

Stevie Ray & Booker T

One word can be used to describe Harlem Heat... MENACING. Brothers Stevie Ray and Booker T grew up on the rough streets of Harlem and their fierce demeanours reflect their difficult upbringing. They quickly learned to look after themselves and have brought that street-smart attitude to WCW.

As physically imposing as any tag team in wrestling history, Harlem Heat have already established themselves as one of the roughest and toughest duos in WCW. When they hired Sister Sherri as their manager, it paid instant dividends as the devious she-witch interfered to gain the WCW World Tag Team Championship for her men.

They hate everyone and during their spare time they make the occasional trip back to their 'hood, just to keep themselves in touch with the lifestyle that has made them the force they are today.

PROFILE

Height: 6' 5" & 6' 2"
Weight: 291lbs & 258lbs
Birthday: August 22 & March 1
Hometown: Harlem, NY
Signature Manoeuvre: Heat Bomb
WCW Titles Held: WCW World Tag Team Champions 1/95, 6/95

WCW TITLES

Ric Flair

Sting

Steve Austin

Vader

CHAMPIONS

WCW WORLD HEAVYWEIGHT CHAMPIONS

11/27/87	Ric Flair def. Ron Garvin
02/20/89	Ricky Steamboat
05/07/89	Ric Flair
07/07/90	Sting
01/11/91	Ric Flair
07/01/91	VACANT
07/14/91	Lex Luger def. Barry Windham
02/29/92	Sting
07/12/92	Vader
08/03/92	Ron Simmons
12/30/92	Vader
03/11/93	Sting
03/17/93	Vader
12/27/93	Ric Flair
07/17/94	Hulk Hogan

Hulk Hogan

Jim Duggan

WCW UNITED STATES CHAMPIONS

05/13/88	Barry Windham def. Nikita Koloff for vacant title
02/20/89	Lex Luger
05/07/89	Michael Hayes
05/22/89	Lex Luger
10/27/90	Stan Hansen
12/16/90	Lex Luger
07/14/91	VACANT
08/25/91	Sting def. Steve Austin
11/19/91	Rick Rude
01/11/93	Dustin Rhodes defeats Ricky Steamboat after title is stripped from Rude
05/93	VACANT
08/30/93	Dustin Rhodes def. Rick Rude
12/27/93	Steve Austin
08/24/94	Ricky Steamboat
09/18/94	Steve Austin awarded belt after Steamboat cannot defend due to injury
09/18/94	Hacksaw Jim Duggan
12/27/94	Vader
03/25/95	VACANT
06/18/95	Sting defeats Meng in Tournament Final

WCW TITLES

Harlem Heat

Steiners

Hol

Lord Regal

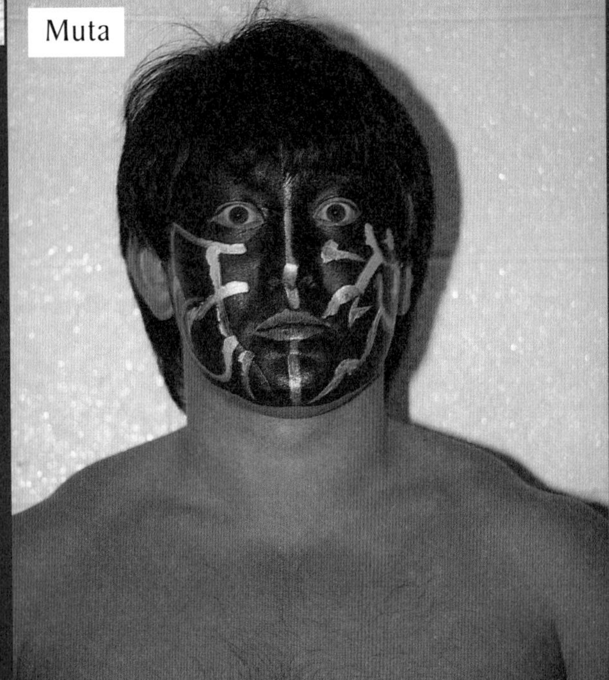
Muta

Road

CHAMPIONS

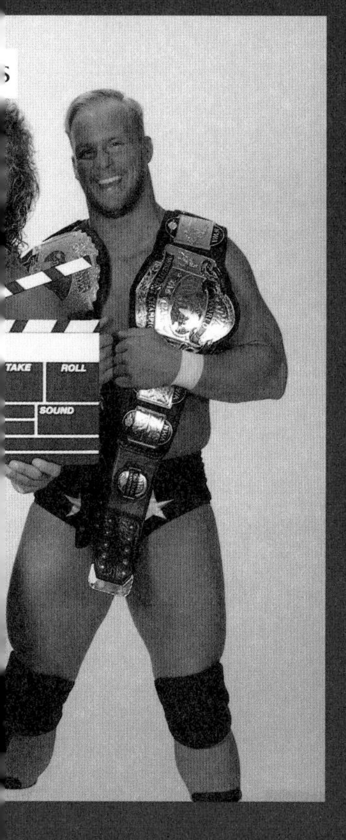

WCW WORLD TELEVISION CHAMPIONS

01/26/88	Mike Rotunda def. Nikita Koloff
12/26/88	Rick Steiner
02/20/89	Mike Rotunda
03/31/89	Sting
09/03/89	Great Muta
01/02/90	Arn Anderson
12/04/90	Z-Man
01/14/91	Arn Anderson
05/19/91	Bobby Eaton
06/13/91	Steve Austin
04/27/92	Barry Windham
05/23/92	Steve Austin
09/02/92	Ricky Steamboat
09/29/92	Scott Steiner
12/92	VACANT
03/02/93	Paul Orndorff def. Erik Watts
08/18/93	Ricky Steamboat
09/19/93	Lord Steven Regal
06/02/94	Larry Zbyszko
06/23/94	Lord Steven Regal
09/18/94	Johnny B. Badd
01/08/95	Arn Anderson
06/18/95	Renegade

WCW WORLD TAG TEAM CHAMPIONS

03/27/88	Windham & Luger defeat Anderson & Blanchard
04/20/88	Anderson & Blanchard
09/10/88	Midnight Express
10/29/88	Road Warriors
02/04/89	Williams & Rotunda
05/07/89	VACANT
06/14/89	Fabulous Freebirds
01/11/89	Steiners
05/19/90	Doom
02/24/91	Fabulous Freebirds
03/09/91	Steiners
06/91	VACANT
09/05/91	Anderson & Zbyszko def. Rick Steiner & Kazmaier
11/19/91	Steamboat & Rhodes
01/16/92	Anderson & Eaton
05/03/92	Steiners
07/05/92	Gordy & Williams
09/21/92	Windham & Rhodes
11/18/92	Steamboat & Douglas
03/02/93	Hollywood Blonds
08/18/93	Anderson & Roma
09/19/93	Nasty Boys
10/23/93	Scorpio & Bagwell
10/24/93	Nasty Boys
05/22/94	Cactus Jack & Sullivan
07/17/94	Pretty Wonderful
09/26/94	Stars & Stripes
10/23/94	Pretty Wonderful
11/16/94	Stars & Stripes
01/14/95	Harlem Heat
05/21/95	Nasty Boys
06/28/95	Harlem Heat

WCW WCW WCW WCW WCW WCW WCW WCW
SPRING
WCW
WCW WCW WCW WCW WCW WCW WCW WCW